ROUTER
A CRAFTSMAN'S GUIDE

ROUTER

A CRAFTSMAN'S GUIDE

ALAN GOODSELL

THE GUILD OF MASTER CRAFTSMAN PUBLICATIONS

First published 2013 by
Guild of Master Craftsman Publications Ltd
Castle Place, 166 High Street, Lewes,
East Sussex BN7 1XU

This title has been created with material first published
in *Router: A Craftsman's Guide* (2010)

ISBN 978-1-86108-901-4

A catalog record for this book is available from the
British Library.

Editor Nicola Hodgson
Designer Simon Goggin
Illustrator Simon Rodway

Set in Din

Color origination by GMC Reprographics
Printed in China

Acknowledgments
Special thanks to:
Infinity Cutting Tools
Grizzly Industrial
Makita USA
Ana Maria Benitez, Alan Goodsell's assistant
Alberto Sanciprian, set builder

CONTENTS

INTRODUCTION 8

ANATOMY OF A ROUTER 9
ROUTER BITS AND CUTS 16
EIGHT RULES 25

TECHNIQUE 1 STRAIGHT EDGING
AND TRIMMING 32
TECHNIQUE 2 BISCUIT JOINING 37
TECHNIQUE 3 DADOS 43
TECHNIQUE 4 RABBETS 50
TECHNIQUE 5 SMALL CIRCLES 53
TECHNIQUE 6 MORTISE AND TENON 58
TECHNIQUE 7 EDGE MOLDING 69
TECHNIQUE 8 LARGE CIRCLES 76

PROJECT 1 ENTERTAINMENT UNIT
FOR FLATSCREEN TV 82
PROJECT 2 ROUND TABLE 90
SAFETY ADVICE 97

GLOSSARY 100
INDEX 102

INTRODUCTION

A router is, without a doubt, the most versatile woodworking power tool there is. With a router, and a careful selection of router bits and jigs, a craftsman will be able to carry out almost any woodworking task. This means that routing is an economical investment, as only a little money needs to be spent on tools and equipment. A workshop full of power tools and machinery would set you back a fair amount of money, not to mention the space that you would need to house it all. With the routing approach to woodworking, the router is the single most expensive investment; router bits are relatively inexpensive, and jigs can be easily made from scrap wood in the store.

I aim to show a craftsman with any level of skill that with this modest investment in tools a lot of work can be achieved and some truly impressive things can be made. A plunge router was selected for this book, as this style is more versatile than its fixed-base cousin, and there are plenty of them available in all major stores.

Essentially, any woodworking project is created by using a number of different woodworking techniques, and this is what I've based this book on: routing techniques. The collection of techniques I demonstrate can be added together to complete any number of woodworking projects. You may wish to follow them exactly as they are presented here, or modify them to suit your purposes or projects.

Router bits are fundamental to routing, and it is they that do all the cutting work. Carefully selecting the ones for your collection will greatly depend on what you want to achieve and make. If you were to get all the router bits featured here it would be a tremendous start, and give you hours of woodworking activity.

There are plenty of places to buy off-the-shelf jigs and templates for the router, and many of them are very good value for money, while others are even essential; a clamping straight edge is one that is thoroughly recommended. For many tasks, though, you may want to consider making them yourself, as they can often be constructed from scraps and offcuts from previous projects, or even an inexpensive purchase from your local home store.

While you are in the home store, check out the types of wood they have. You will see that the projects featured are made from manmade wood boards that are inexpensive. You can choose to finish them in their natural wood state or color and paint them to suit your décor.

The most important mission here is to have fun with your routing, and end up with something you have made that is unique and you are proud of.

Happy routing.

Alan Goodsell

WOODWORKING SAFETY

Woodworking is an inherently dangerous pastime and many safety precautions must be taken when using both hand and power tools. Always read the instructions supplied with your tools and follow all tool manufacturers' safety advice. Make sure that you use the safety devices supplied with your tools. To illustrate some processes clearly, we may show operations with these devices removed. Do not follow this example and always adhere to manufacturers' instructions. Always work within your limits and do not attempt a woodworking process that you are unsure of. I hope you enjoy your woodworking, but must stress that safety is the most important consideration.

ANATOMY OF A ROUTER

A router is a complex power tool with some particular components that are useful to identify. The router featured is the plunge router, as opposed to its cousin, the fixed-base router. The plunge router is more versatile than other variants, and although some routers will look different, most of the component terminology will be the same.

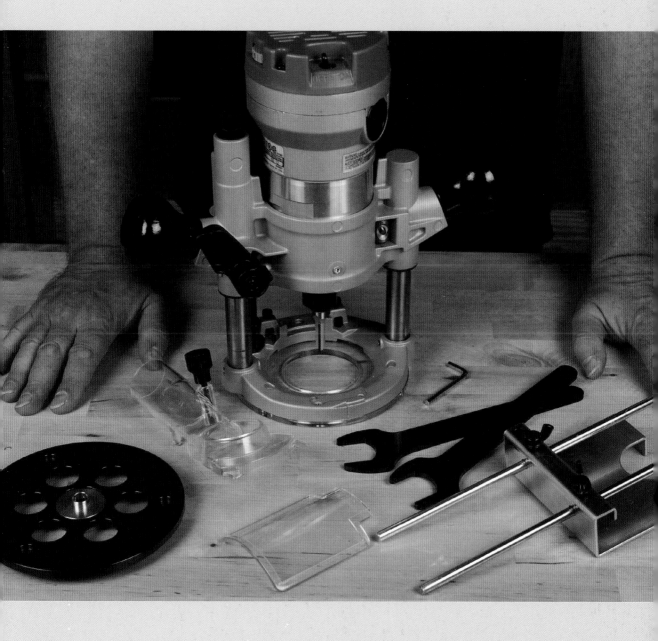

FRONT OF A PLUNGE ROUTER

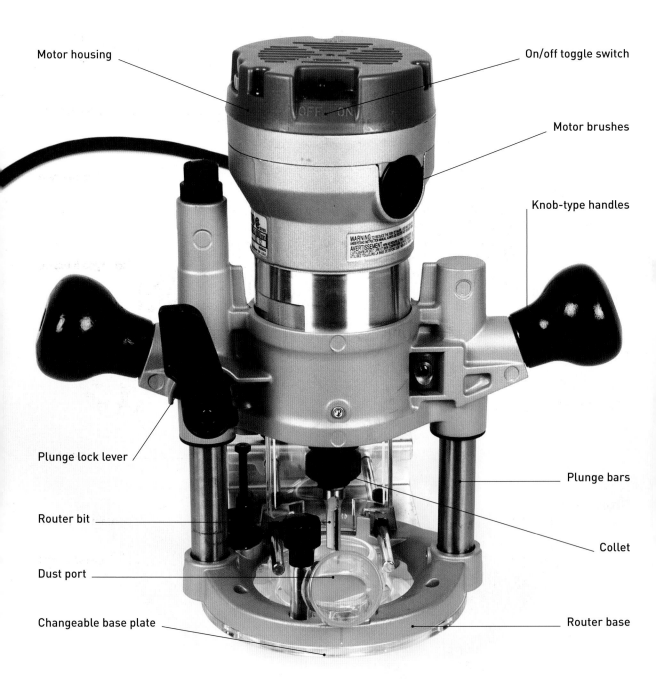

Motor housing

On/off toggle switch

Motor brushes

Knob-type handles

Plunge lock lever

Plunge bars

Router bit

Collet

Dust port

Changeable base plate

Router base

BACK OF A PLUNGE ROUTER

Motor housing

Air vents

Power cord

Speed control

Speed scale

Motor brushes

Knob-type handles

Chip deflector

Plunge bars

Straight fence

Depth stop rod

Capstan turret

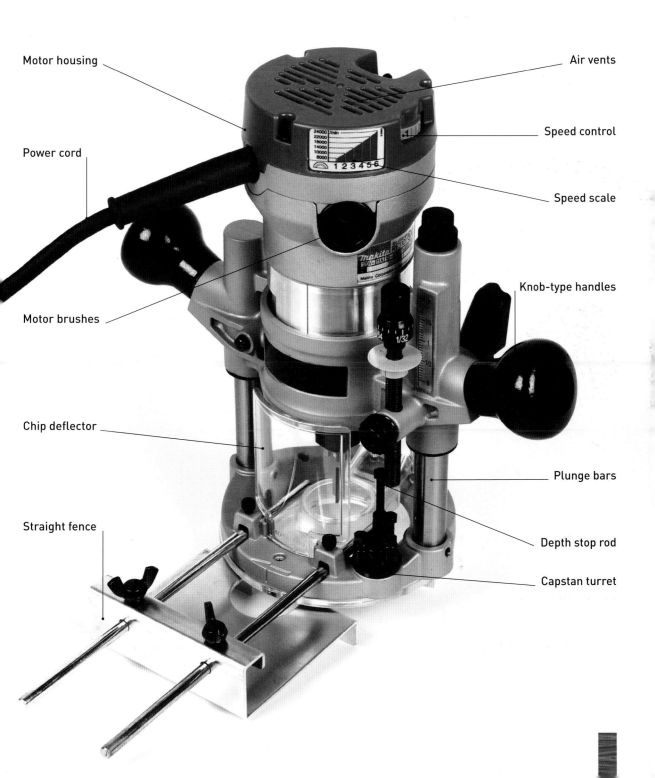

The base of the router holds the router bit at right angles and a precise distance from the wood to enable accurate cuts.

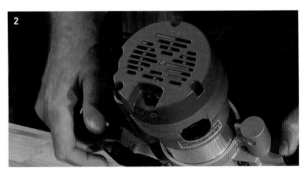

The motor body houses the router's electric motor, which will typically spin at up to 25,000 revs per minute.

Take care not to block the airflow through the vents; this may lead to overheating, which will inevitably shorten the life of your router.

The gyroscopic action when the motor is running can feel a little strange at first, as the router tries to stay in position when you try to turn it.

The handles of a router are critically important, as they are your only means of making a router go where, and when, you want it to.

Knob-type handles can be used from any angle and, although they sacrifice ergonomic comfort in one position, they are usable in any position.

On plunge routers with knob-type handles, the on/off switch tends to be on the top of the motor housing, and will be of the toggle type.

A wheel on the router's motor body controls the speed of the motor; it is usually numbered for speed settings.

A plunge router has the ability to quickly and easily set depth of cut. This is done via the plunge mechanism. Here it is at the top...

...and here the router is fully plunged. The height can be locked in place using the locking mechanism, controlled by the large lever on the front.

The capstan turret is a multi-depth stop device that can be quickly rotated for the speedy use of preset depth settings.

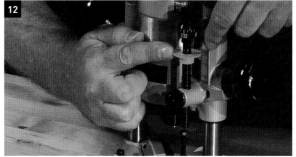

The depth rod has an end that bears on the stops of the capstan and is quickly set using the locking nut or wheel.

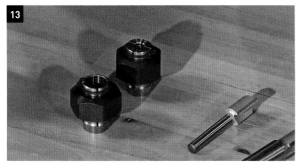

The collet is the split-collar device that holds the router bit securely to the router. Insert the bit into the collet...

...and make sure that at least three-quarters of the router bit's shank is in the collet, but also ensure that it does not bottom out.

Tighten the collet so it holds the router bit's shank securely. Make sure it is tight enough to hold, but not so tight that it might damage the threads.

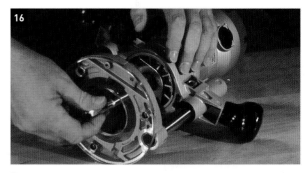

To remove the bit, simply do the reverse of tightening, but run the nut until it is tight again and then loosen it some more with the wrench.

This fence allows you to set a cut at a precise distance from the edge of a workpiece by sliding the router and keeping the fence tight to the edge of the workpiece.

Fit the fence to the mounting points on the router's base and tighten in place. Adjust the position of the fence and secure it in position using its plastic knobs.

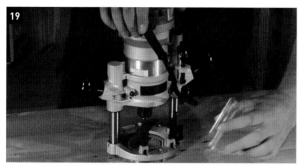

A chip deflector helps to direct larger chips away from you. It clips into place on the router base, and can be used with or without the dust port.

The chip deflector is transparent—otherwise it would obscure your view of the router bit.

A dust port simply clips into the router's base and encloses the router bit. It is also transparent so that it does not obscure your vision of the router bit cutting.

The dust port attaches to your shop dust extractor. It can drastically reduce the amount of dust in the air when you are routing.

Most routers have alternative bases. The standard one fitted is transparent, with a large opening that is ideal for general use.

An optional base is available that has an opening to fit standard template guides. Plenty of other base options are available depending on your requirements.

ROUTER BITS AND CUTS

Router bits come in many shapes and sizes, and their wide variety of profiles allows them to perform a large number of different tasks. It is important to know how they are made, and what makes a good router bit, so that you can make an informed purchase. You also need to know how to look after your bits to ensure they cut well.

Router bits come in many forms, so you will be able to find one for exactly the purpose you need. As varied as they are, they all have some common features.

The shank of the router bit is the accurately ground part that the router's collet holds on to.

Router bits have shanks in two common sizes: half-inch and quarter-inch diameter (12mm and 6mm). The larger the shank, the more robust the bit will be.

Here you can see the difference in size between a half-inch (12mm) and a quarter-inch (6mm) shank and the collets they fit into.

Each size shank must be installed into the correct size collet. It is better to use correctly sized collets with small bits than to use reduction sleeves.

Larger shank bits generally vibrate less and provide better cuts. However, you may need a small shank bit for small-diameter cuts.

The router bit's shank is held securely in the collet. A good tip is to have at least three-quarters of the shank in the collet, but make sure it doesn't bottom out.

The body of the router bit is designed to provide the maximum support to the cutting tip.

The carbide tip is brazed to the router bit's body in the gullet that is machined to receive it.

The gullet is cut so that the side that does not carry the tip performs the task of a chipbreaker.

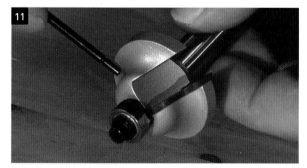

A shear cutting angle is formed by the gullet; this will give a superior cut and help to remove waste chips.

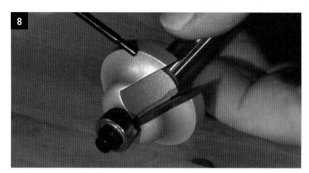

It is possible to hone the cutting tips of a bit to restore a sharp edge—here I used a diamond hone—although this must be done with care.

STRAIGHT BITS

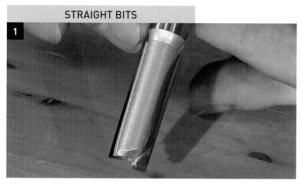

Straight bits are the most common type of router bit. They are available in a wide range of diameters.

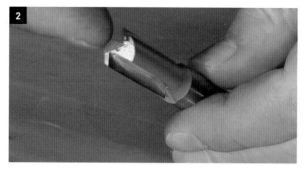

Some straight bits have the ability to plunge cut, while others do not. Ones that cut on the end have an extra cutting tip on the end of the bit.

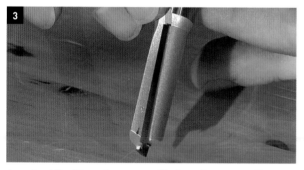

A router bit with a shear cut will give a better-quality cut. A rule of thumb with straight bits is that a maximum depth of cut should not exceed the diameter of the bit.

Solid carbide bits are available in different versions. This up-cut version will be good for leaving a clean edge on the bottom of your work.

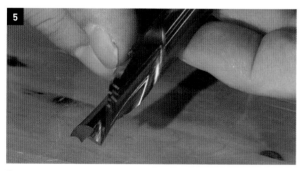

This down-cut version will give you a clean cut on the top of your work.

This dual-purpose bit with an up and down cut will give a good edge on both the top and bottom of your work. It must be positioned centrally to achieve this.

DADO BITS

A good-quality dado bit will have downshear to give a good edge on the top corners of the dado.

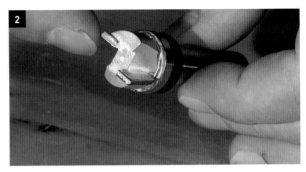

The cutting tips are sharp on the end so you get a clean, square cut in the bottom of the dado.

A top-mounted bearing on the shank of the dado bit is exactly the same diameter as the bit itself, so will make using fences very simple.

The dado bit is used vertically. If the bit is not the same size as the piece of wood that needs to fit in the dado, a second cut will be required.

RABBET BITS

These rabbet bits are used to create an accurate step in a piece of wood—for example, to fit a back panel in the rear of a carcass.

The up-shear cut will give a good finish in the bottom of the rabbet.

These bits come in a range of sizes. Fitting different-size bearings will give a selection of cutting widths for rabbets.

The end cut of the cutting tip in relation to the bearing is what gives the rabbet cut.

PATTERN BITS

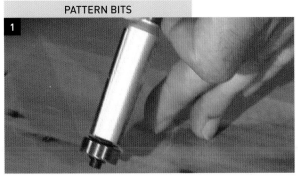

Pattern bits are part of the straight bit family, but a spigot is formed on the end onto which a bearing is placed.

Bearings can be replaced, but make sure they are bolted on tightly before use. Note the down-shear cut, which will give a good edge on the top of the work.

The bearing is the same diameter as the cutting diameter of the bit. It runs on a pattern or template to ensure the router bit reproduces it exactly.

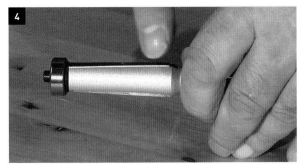

Inspect the cutter's tip before use; it is possible to wear down a portion of the tip if it is used repeatedly in the same place on manmade materials.

EDGE-MOLDING BITS

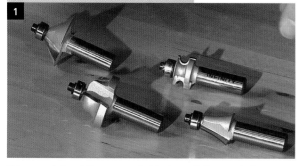

Edge-molding bits are available in a plethora of shapes to create almost any molding—check out router bit catalogs or the internet.

The molding is formed by the precisely ground edge of the bit.

In most cases, the molding is positioned by a bearing on the end of the bit. The depth of the molding is set by the router's depth setting.

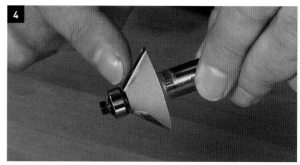

This is a chamfer bit, which will be used often as it is a versatile molding to tidy up edges.

An edge bead bit is useful for making the edge of table or chair rails look attractive.

A Queen Anne molding is a good choice to decorate the edges of tabletops or countertops.

BISCUIT BITS

1 The router is a versatile tool that can sometimes replace other power tools; in this case, the biscuit joiner.

2 The biscuit-joining bit or cutter is a slot cutter; the correct thickness for a biscuit-joining plate, mounted on an arbor.

3 On the end of the arbor is a bearing; this can be changed according to the size of the biscuit plate that is required.

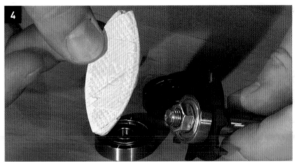

4 The small bearing will set the cutter's depth of cut to suit the large number 20 size of biscuit plate.

5 The larger bearing will set the cutter's depth of cut to suit the small number 0 size biscuit plate.

6 The router is an ideal tool for biscuit joining, as it has a base that is at right angles to the cut of the biscuit cutter and is infinitely adjustable for depth.

ROUTER BIT PROFILES

Shown here are some of the many router bit profiles available. They are also the ones that are shown in use within the Techniques section (see pages 32–76).

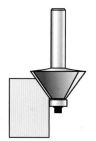

Chamfer bit

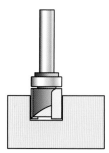

Dado bit

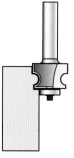

Edge bead bit

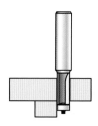

Pattern bit

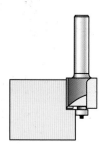

Rabbet bit

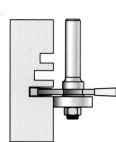

Biscuit joining bit

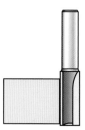

Straight bit

Queen Anne bit

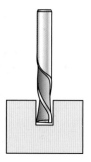

Downcut spiral
straight bit

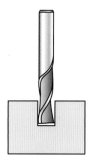

Upcut spiral
straight bit

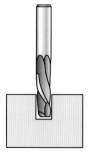

Up and downcut
spiral straight bit

EIGHT RULES

Routing is a very versatile woodworking procedure, but some useful rules will help you to be safe and to achieve the most satisfying woodworking experience possible. Some readily available, inexpensive products will be needed to accomplish this. Follow these guidelines and you will quickly learn some good routing habits that will last a lifetime.

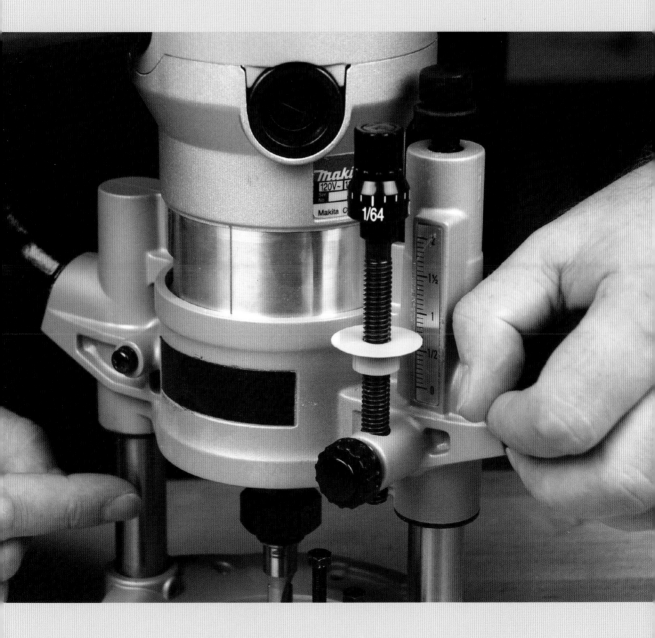

RULE 1: SHARP BITS

A sharp bit will produce good cuts, but over time it will dull with use.

Inspect the router bit's cutting tips to see if there is any damage or wear. It is usually possible to feel a dull edge with your finger, but take care not to cut yourself.

If the router bit's edge feels dull, it is possible to bring back a sharp edge with a diamond hone. Rub the hone on the inside edge of a cutting tip...

...and then turn the router bit over and repeat the process on the other tip. Ensure that you make the same number of strokes on each tip to keep the bit balanced.

RULE 2: CLEAN BITS & COLLETS

Spray some proprietary cleaning agent onto the router bit to loosen the dust and resin buildup.

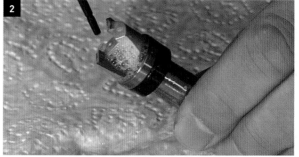

Let the cleaning agent soak for a while, then work off the dust and resin with a soft tool. A piece of wood or plastic stick are good for this, as they won't damage the bit.

Clean the router bit carefully with a cloth—remember that the bit has sharp edges.

Inspect the router bit to make sure all the resin buildup is removed. The bit is ready for use the next time it is needed, and it will perform well now it is clean.

Spray the collet with a proprietary cleaning agent to loosen up any dust and resin buildup.

Let the cleaning agent soak, then clean it out with a brush that is small enough to pass through the collet.

Gun-cleaning brushes are a good choice; they are inexpensive, readily available, and the brush is made of brass, which is soft enough not to damage the collet...

...but stiff enough to clean inside the collet thoroughly. Inspect the collet to make sure it is clean. It will now grip the router bit's shank well.

RULE 3: PRE-FLIGHT CHECK

Checking over the router before use is a good idea as it will uncover anything that may make it unsafe or produce poor cuts. Ensure the switches work properly.

Check the plunge action to make sure there is full and free movement. It is worth applying a coat of thin oil to keep the plunge legs in good condition.

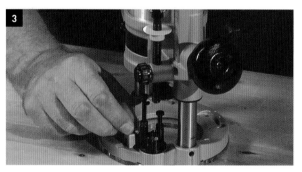

Make sure there are no loose nuts, bolts, or anything that may come adrift while using the router and pose a threat if sucked into the router bit.

Check the spindle for runout. If the spindle is bent, the router will produce vibration and a poor cut. It can be replaced, but this is generally the end of the router's life.

Inspect the power cable to see if there are any nicks or cuts. If there are, have the cable replaced by a qualified electrician to avoid shocks.

Check the plug to make sure it is in good condition and that the pins aren't bent.

RULE 4: HOLDING WORK SECURELY

Holding work securely while routing is a must. There are many clamps available, but a few simple ones will do. These wooden ones are cheap and easy to use.

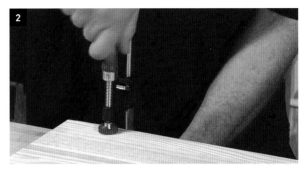

These metal ratchet types are also inexpensive and are very versatile as they come in different lengths. The soft jaws help to avoid marking the workpiece.

A router mat is one of the simplest holding devices out there. It is a slightly sticky mat that will prevent the work from moving laterally.

If the mat is not enough on its own, use a weightlifting dumbbell to give some extra down pressure. A pair of 15lb (6.8kg) weights are a good set to get.

RULE 5: CLEAN WORK AREA

While setting up for a routing cut, it is possible to accumulate tools and marking devices that will be in the way of your routing.

Make sure to tidy all these away so they aren't in the path of the router while cutting.

RULE 6: PRACTICE BEFORE CUTTING

Once your work area is clear, it is a good idea to make a practice cut with the router switched off to make sure that you have a good stance throughout the cut.

Start at one end of the cut and move the router towards you, against the direction the bit is rotating (see page 75).

Move the router through the middle of the path of the cut...

...all the way to the end of the path of the cut. This will help you to stand in the correct position and not be overbalanced at any point.

RULE 7: DUST EXTRACTION

Cutting wood with a router will produce a lot of dust and debris. Apart from wearing safety equipment it is preferable to use a shop vacuum.

A good type has a built-in feature that turns the shop vacuum on and off when you turn the router on and off.

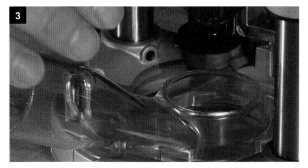

If your router doesn't have one built in, attach a dust port to the router's base.

Plug the hose from the shop vacuum into the dust port; the amount of dust that is sucked away is remarkable.

RULE 8: MEASURE TWICE, CUT ONCE

Wood is a valuable commodity and a wrong cut will consign it to the scrap bin. Make sure you cut right the first time by measuring carefully.

Measure and mark a line from the scale on the measuring tape...

...move the tape away and then measure your line again to confirm that it is in the correct place. You are then safe to proceed with marking a line.

Feel confident that you are marking the cutting line in the correct place, as you have double-checked its position.

TECHNIQUE 1
STRAIGHT EDGING AND TRIMMING

Dimensioning boards and cutting straight edges are important for the accurate construction of cabinets and the basis for precise woodworking. With a router, a straight bit, and a straight edge you can easily and precisely perform this task, which is the mainstay of woodworking.

Fit a good-sized straight bit in the router. A half-inch diameter (12mm) one is a good choice.

Measure the distance between the tip of the router bit and the edge of the router's base.

Mark down this measurement for future reference. A piece of scrap wood makes a convenient notepad.

Clamp your work securely to the bench so it does not slide around while being routed.

Mark the position on one side of where you want to trim your work to...

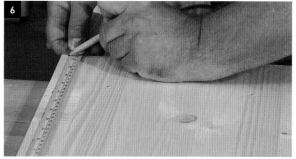

...taking care to make the pencil mark clear.

Repeat the measurement on the other side of your work...

...also making sure that the mark is easily visible.

Then, using a rule, place a mark back from your previous mark the distance from the router bit's tip to the edge of the router's base that you wrote down.

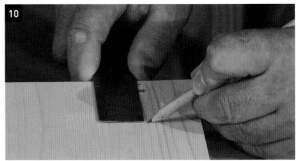

Repeat this on the other side of your work. These are the marks that you will line up your clamp with.

Place a piece of scrap wood on the exit edge of your work so the clamp will hold that too.

Position the clamp on your work and slide the jaws into place.

Jiggle the clamp around so that it lines up exactly with your marks.

Then depress the clamping lever to secure the clamp on your work.

Try to move the clamp to ensure it is held securely. Also check to see that it hasn't moved off the marks while being tightened up.

Plunge the router to depth and place it on the end of your work with the router's base against the clamp.

Move the router toward you and make the cut.

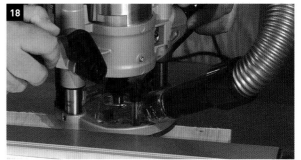

Carry on cutting all along the edge of your work...

...until you reach the end. Make sure that you cut into the piece of scrap wood that you clamped there.

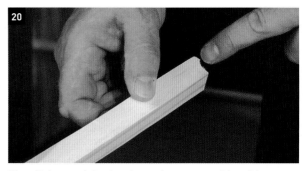

The slight notch in the piece of scrap wood is evidence that the cut has been performed properly.

Here you can see in detail the effect of the piece of wood (chipbreaker) to eliminate any tearout on the end of the workpiece.

When the cut is finished, let the router stop and set it down in a safe place.

Use a steel rule to run along the edge you have just cut.

This will show that the cut is straight and true, as well as being at exact right angles to the face of your work.

BISCUIT JOINING

Joining boards together was simplified with the invention of the biscuit joiner, as it became possible to quickly align and join them either in line or at right angles with slots and flat plates called biscuits. Now it is possible to achieve this task with just a router, a pencil, and an inexpensive slot-cutting bit.

Line up the pieces of wood to be joined and decide how many biscuits will fit.

In this case it is three, so mark their centerlines.

Position one...

...two and...

...three.

Next, install a biscuit cutter in the router. Make sure that the cutter has the correct-size bearing fitted to match the size of the biscuit being used.

Plunge the router to the depth you want the biscuits set at. The center of the wood thickness is typically the best place.

Adjust and lock the depth controls on the router so that the depth of cut is repeatable and accurate.

Start the router and plunge to the depth you have set.

Once the router is at the correct depth, make sure the base is stable on the wood. Perform the cut to the cutter's bearing, and centered on the pencil line.

Make the first cut. When the cutter is running on the bearing, move it laterally to make sure the slot is wide enough to receive the biscuit.

While the router is running, move the cutter away from the wood and relocate it at the next pencil line.

Repeat this process on the second slot position.

Then move onto the third cut to complete the cutting on the end of the board.

Deplunge the router and move it to a safe place before proceeding with the next process.

The next step is to cut the slots in the vertical board. Clamp it securely to the bench and then place the router on top.

Plunge the router to your preset depth settings. This will ensure that the joints line up exactly.

Start the router and proceed to make the first cut centered on the pencil line, and to the depth set by the bearing.

Move the bit laterally to make the slot the correct size for the biscuit.

Move the cutter to the position of the second cut...

...and then on to complete cutting the third slot.

Deplunge the router, let it stop, and set it down in a safe place.

It is a good idea to set out the biscuits and assemble the joint without glue so that you can try out the fit.

Place the biscuits in the slots of one board...

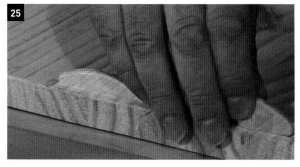

...until all three are in position, making sure they are centered on the pencil lines.

Once they are in place, the other board can be dry-fitted.

Position the board over the biscuits, making sure its pencil lines are in alignment.

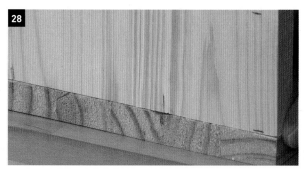

Press the two boards together and the biscuits will align them perfectly on their face. Slide the board laterally to make sure it lines up on the end.

If you run your finger along the face where the two boards join, you will see they are perfectly flush.

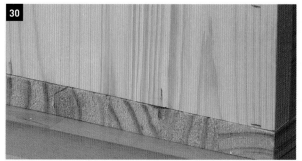

When you are satisfied with the joint, take it apart and proceed to glue it up. Be sparing with the glue, as it will squeeze out of the joint.

TECHNIQUE 3
DADOS

Dados are simply square-bottomed grooves cut into a piece of wood that another piece of wood will fit into at right angles. They are the joint of choice for fitting shelves or dividers into cabinets or shelf units, and the front of the joint can be hidden for a clean, joint-free look. All that is needed to create them is a router, a dado bit, and a straight edge.

Install the dado bit in the router. The bit has a bearing that will follow a straight edge.

Clamp your work securely to a bench, ensuring that the clamps are clear of the working path of the router.

Measure the distance from the edge of the router bit to the edge of the router's base. Record the measurement.

The dado will run across the work, so measure and mark the position of the dado on one side of the work...

...and repeat the measurement on the other side.

It is worth checking the pencil marks to make sure that you haven't made any measuring errors.

From the position lines, mark the measurement that you previously recorded—this is the distance from the bit edge to the base edge.

First mark one side...

...and then mark the other side. These are the marks that the straight edge will line up with.

Place the straight edge on the work...

...carefully line it up with the pencil marks...

...and lock it in position.

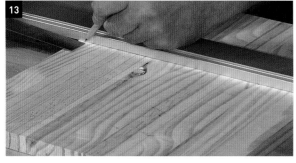

The dado will stop short of the edge of the work, so make a mark at the position where the step will be.

Make sure the pencil mark is clear enough so you can see it while routing.

After setting the depth of the cut with the depth stop and capstan turret, place the router on the work.

Turn on the router and line up the edge of the base with the straight edge.

Plunge the router to depth and proceed to make the cut.

Make the cut slowly and carefully, making sure that you keep the router's base tight against the straight edge.

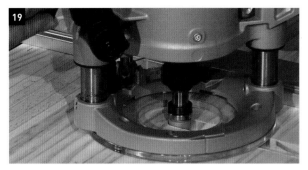

Continue cutting the dado without stopping...

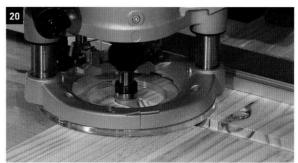

...until you reach the pencil mark that denotes the end of the cut.

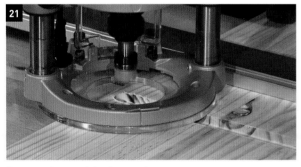

Stop cutting and deplunge the router.

Then turn the router off and move it out of the way.

Next, check that the piece of wood or shelf to fit into the dado actually does fit. If not, you will have to reposition the fence and make another cut to make it wider.

The shelf will need a step cut into the end of it, so push it in the dado until it bottoms out.

Then mark the depth of the dado on the shelf.

Line up the edge of the shelf with the carcass edge and mark the position of the end of the dado.

It is best to mark the step at the place where the radius of the cut starts to narrow. This makes it easier to line up the edges of the carcass.

Clamp the shelf securely in a vise.

Using a handsaw, carefully cut to the depth line...

...making sure the cut is even on both sides of the board.

Turn the shelf round in the vise and clamp it securely.

Using the handsaw, complete the cut...

...sawing down to the previous cut to produce the step.

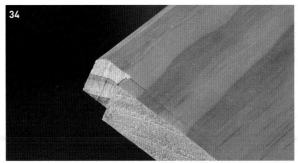

The step should be squarely cut accurately to the lines.

Line up the edges of the shelf and carcass and push the joint together.

Once together, the shelf and carcass side form a strong load-bearing joint. Repeat the process on all the dados you need, then glue and assemble the carcass.

TECHNIQUE 4
RABBETS

Rabbets are an edge groove mostly used for fitting backs into cabinets. The rabbet will hide the edges of the back so it can't be seen from the ends of the cabinet. Rabbet bits come in many sizes, or with a number of different diameter bearings, so you will easily find one that is perfect for your project.

Install the rabbet bit in the router. The bit has a bearing that will follow the edge of your work.

Make sure your work is held securely. In this case, a router mat and weight are sufficient.

Set the depth of cut on the router so that the rabbet is the correct depth.

Position the router on the end of the work, plunge to depth, and proceed to cut the rabbet.

The rabbet bit makes a clean cut, but take care to keep the bearing against the work to ensure an even rabbet.

Continue cutting the rabbet the full length of the work.

When the end of the rabbet cut is reached...

...deplunge the router...

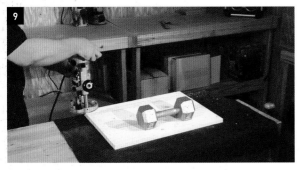

...turn it off and move it safely away.

In this instance, the rabbet is to house the back of a carcass, so place the back in the rabbet to test the fit.

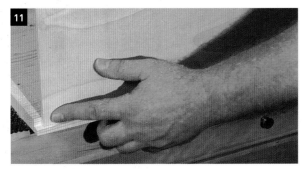

The rabbet can be positioned to suit your requirements. Check to see if the fit is what is required. If not, reset the depth and cut again.

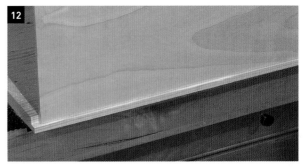

Cut the rabbet in all the carcass parts to complete the process.

SMALL CIRCLES

Cutting small circles is a useful technique when you need to create holes for cable management, for example. For this task all you need is a router, a straight bit, and an easy-to-make jig. It is then possible to repeatedly create the exact same size hole. Make a selection of different-size hole jigs so they are always ready for use when needed.

A simple jig will need to be made: this is just a piece of plywood with the size of hole to be reproduced accurately cut into it.

Mark out the hole by drawing round a can, or use a pair of school compasses. Then, using a jigsaw, carefully cut out the hole.

When the hole is cut, file and sand it so it is smooth and to the lines. Positioning it over a vise will keep it steady and give good access.

Finish sanding the hole in the jig with fine sandpaper to make a good surface for the router bit's bearing to run on.

The lines that mark the center of the hole will be useful for positioning the jig where you want it on your work.

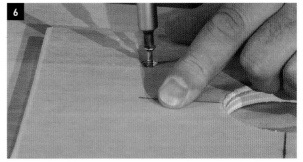

Screw the jig to the work and make sure the screw holes are on the side of the work that won't be seen.

Although the attachment method used here is screwing, it is also possible to use some heavy-duty double-sided tape to hold the jig in place.

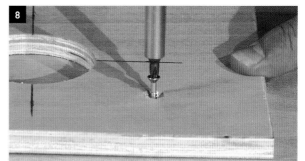

With the first screw tight, position the jig exactly in place and tighten the second screw.

The dado bit is used for this job as it has a flush bearing and a bottom cut.

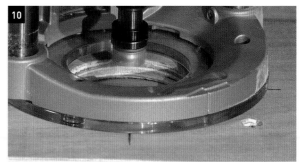

Plunge the bit into the jig; the bearing will run on the cut-out hole to reproduce it exactly.

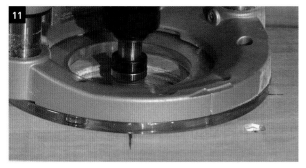

It may not be possible to make the cut in one go, so run the bit around the jig...

...then set the router to cut deeper...

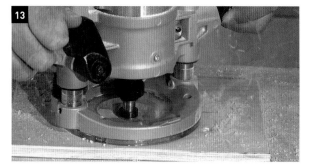

...and repeat until the hole is cut all the way through the wood.

Retract the router bit and move the router carefully to a safe place.

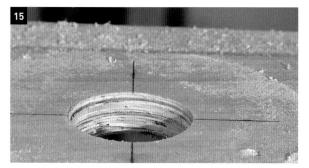

The cut made with the dado bit will be nice and clean, and exactly the same size as the jig.

Remove the jig for the final cleanup.

Although the hole will be smooth, a final sanding is recommended to take off the sharp edges.

It is now possible to repeat cutting the small hole as many times as you want; all the holes will be exactly the same.

SMALL CIRCLE JIG

A simple jig is all that is required to rout small circles.

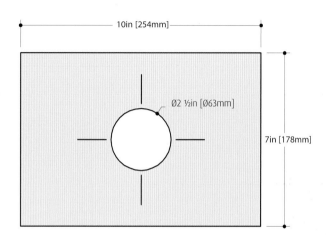

10in [254mm]

Ø2 ½in [Ø63mm]

7in [178mm]

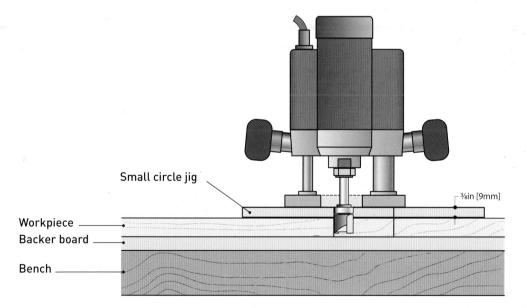

Small circle jig

⅜in [9mm]

Workpiece

Backer board

Bench

Side view of small circle jig in use

MORTISE AND TENON

The mortise-and-tenon joint has been around since the early days of woodworking. It is a simple peg-and-hole joint that is easily created with a router, straight bits, and simple-to-make jigs. This joint is typically used on rail- and stile-type cabinet doors and also to create strong joints on frames.

MORTISE

A mortise is a slot that acts as a socket for the tenon. A straight bit is installed in the router for this procedure.

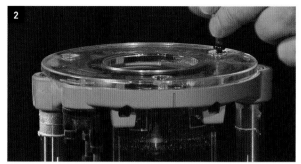

A jig that requires a template guide will be used, so the router's base needs to be changed to accommodate this. Unscrew the bolts that hold the standard base...

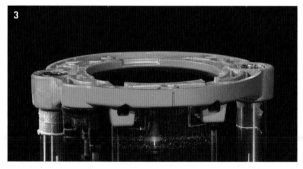

...and remove it in preparation for fitting the one that accepts template guides.

Attach the template-guide base to the router. The template guide is already fitted in the base and is a standard type.

A simple jig needs to be made; this is a piece of plywood with a slot in it to accept the template guide.

The slot runs parallel to the edge of the plywood, which makes it easier to cut using a side fence.

A batten is securely fastened to the underside of the plywood, and at the distance away from the slot that you require the mortise to be routed in the work.

The batten must run parallel with the slot and also be at right angles to the underside of the plywood.

Place the jig on the work.

Then place the two parts in a vise and tighten it securely.

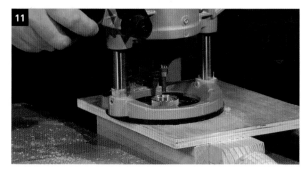

The lateral travel of the router and the resulting length of mortise can be indicated by drawing lines on the jig.

Set the router to the full depth that needs to be cut for the mortise and set one of the capstan stops. Then set as many intermediate stops to get a full depth of cut.

Plunge the router to the first depth—this should be no deeper a cut than the diameter of the bit. Move the router laterally to cut the full length of the mortise.

Reset the depth for the next cut and proceed to route the mortise again, making it deeper.

If an even deeper mortise is required, repeat cutting until the full depth of mortise is achieved.

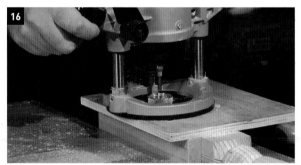

Now deplunge the router, turn it off, and move it to a safe place.

The mortise in now cut, so clear the dust...

...and inspect the mortise. If satisfied, repeat the process and cut all the mortises that are needed.

TENON

A simple jig is needed to guide the router to cut tenons. It is one piece of wood for the router to sit on and guide it.

A batten is attached to it at right angles; this will make sure the router cuts accurate tenons. Set it beyond the end at the length of the tenon.

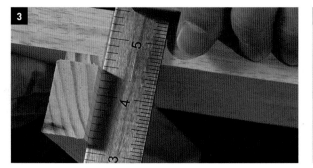

Make sure it is square to the first piece in both directions.

Install a dado bit in the router. This is ideal for tenoning as it is short with an end cut, and has a flush bearing.

Place a rail in the jig and clamp it together. Shown here is a simple clamping system.

Make sure the rail is flush with the end of the batten; this will ensure that the tenon is cut to the correct length.

Set the depth of cut on the router. It will cut the same amount on both sides of the rail and leave a tenon the width of the mortise.

Turn on the router, place it on the jig, and ensure the router-bit bearing is against the jig.

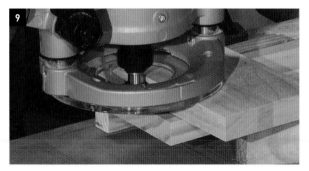

Then start to cut the first side of the tenon, and move the router completely across the rail.

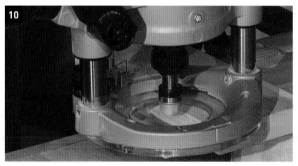

Deplunge the router, switch it off...

...and move it out of harm's way.

Remove the rail and jig from the clamp...

...and flip over the rail and replace it in the jig.

Again, make sure the end of the rail is flush with the end of the jig.

Tighten up the clamp...

...set the router to depth...

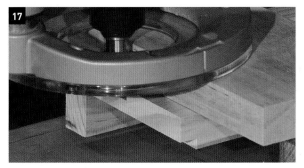

...and make the cut across the full width of the rail.

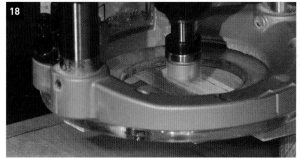

Again, deplunge the router, turn it off, and move it out of the way.

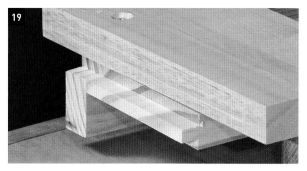

The finished cut has created both sides of the tenon.

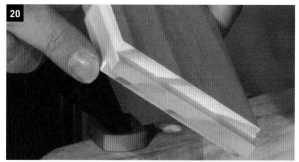

Some trial and error will be required to get the exact size of tenon, so practice cuts on scrap wood. The ends of the tenon need to be trimmed off so it will fit in the mortise.

Use a handsaw to quickly notch out the ends of the tenon.

Make sure your cut is straight and to the same depth on both sides of the rail.

Repeat the process on the other side of the tenon.

It is easier to make the final cuts with the rail laying down in the vise.

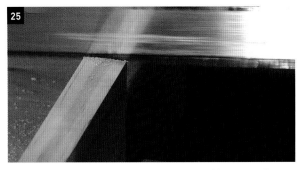

Carefully cut off the end of the tenon, making sure the cut is square.

The finished cut should look like this.

The cutout is on both ends of the tenon.

Place the tenon into the mortise...

...and push together. The joint should be a snug fit, but not too tight—there needs to be room for the glue to spread.

When you are happy with the fit, rout all the tenons and finally glue all the joints together.

MORTISE JIG

Mortises are easy to rout by making and using a simple but accurate jig.

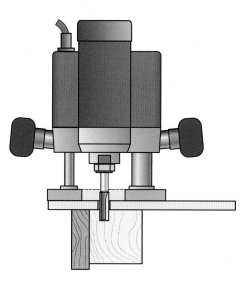

End view of mortise jig in use

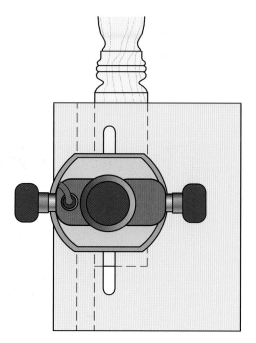

Top view of mortise jig in use

TENON JIG

The tenon is the mating half of the mortise. When accurately routed, the two parts of the mortise and tenon fit snugly together to make a strong joint.

Top view of tenon jig in use

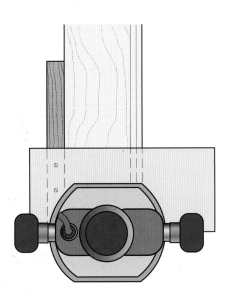

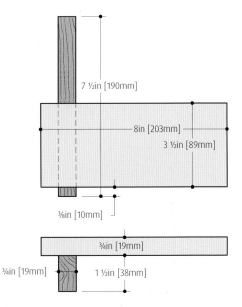

7 ½in [190mm]

8in [203mm]

3 ½in [89mm]

⅜in [10mm]

¾in [19mm]

¾in [19mm]

1 ½in [38mm]

Place the workpiece in the jig and rout one side of the tenon...

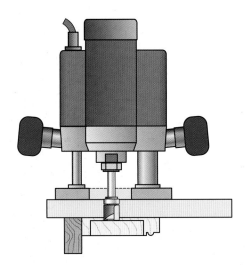

...then turn the workpiece over and rout the other side of the tenon

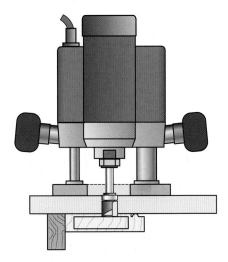

EDGE MOLDING

Decorating the edges of wood with a molding is the most popular task for the router. From the softening of the edge of a table rail to creating the intricate moldings that decorate the edges of table and cabinet tops, the possibilities are as endless as the number of router-bit molding profiles available.

ALONG AN EDGE

Install an edge-molding bit in the router; a bearing-guided edge bead bit is used here.

When routing on the edge of a piece of wood, it is a good idea to clamp all the pieces in a vise to make a broad platform for the router's base.

Set the depth of cut on the router and plunge to depth.

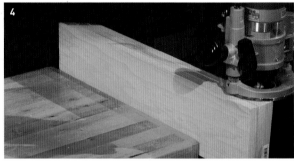

Carefully position the router at the end of the wood and gently start routing, making sure that the molding is fully cut on the end.

Proceed to move the router along the work against the direction of cut of the router bit, making sure the router bit's bearing is tight against the face of the wood.

Continue routing the molding along the wood at a steady pace so the cut is clean...

...until you reach the end. Then check to see that the molding is complete.

Unclamp the workpieces from the vise and reorder them...

...so the piece that has just been molded moves to the back.

Clamp the workpieces tightly in the vise again.

Plunge the router to cut the edge molding on the new piece of wood.

Repeat the process until all the pieces of wood have been edge-molded.

AROUND AN EDGE

Edge-molding bits come in many shapes and sizes. Here a simple chamfer bit is installed in the router.

To route an edge molding around a piece of wood, it is easy to hold the work securely using a weight and a router mat.

Set the router to the depth that is required for the edge molding.

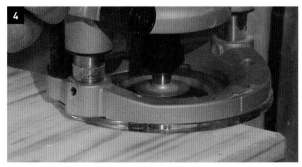

Routing around a piece of wood requires a correct procedure. Start routing across the grain.

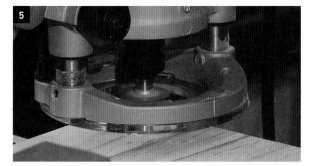

When you reach the end of the cut, make sure that the molding is cut fully.

When cutting across the grain you will notice some tearout on the end of the cut.

Now, turn the work around 90 degrees and hold it down using the weight and mat again.

Route the edge molding along the grain. You will notice that the cut removes the tearout from the first cut.

Continue routing along the edge, keeping the router bit's bearing tight on the wood.

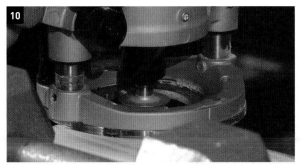

There will not be any tearout at the end of the cut along the grain.

Turn the work 90 degrees again and replace the weight to hold it in place.

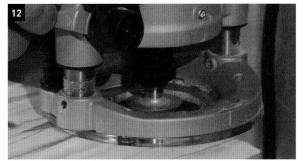

The third cut is made across the grain again.

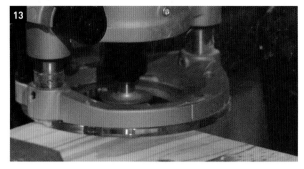

At the end of the cut you will see the familiar tearout produced by an across-the-grain cut.

Rotate the work again 90 degrees for the fourth and final cut.

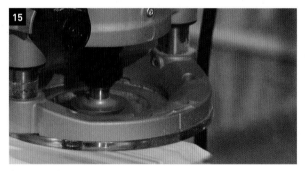

Start routing the edge molding along the grain.

At the end of this last edge-molding cut there is no tearout.

Using this edge-molding cutting procedure ensures that there is no tearout on the molding.

The edge molding is crisp on the corners. This process can be applied to any edge-molding task.

ROUTING EDGE MOLDINGS

Edge moldings can be routed on a workpiece either vertically or horizontally; different techniques are used to create them successfully.

ROUTING A MOLDING ALONG THE EDGE OF A WORKPIECE

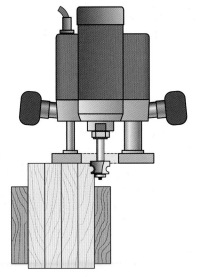 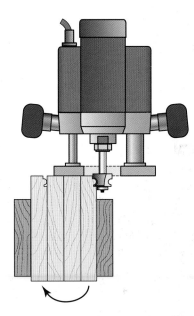

Stack workpieces in a vise to provide support for the router's base

Rout the edge of the first piece then move it to the back of the pile

SEQUENCE OF ROUTING A MOLDING AROUND AN EDGE

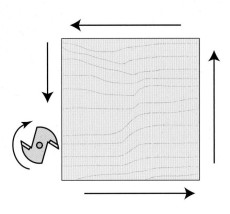

TECHNIQUE 8
LARGE CIRCLES

Cutting large circles in wood with saws can lead to an uneven disaster. Simply attach your router to an easy-to-make jig and cutting them becomes a breeze. The circles can be any size you like and will always be perfectly round—ideal for making round table tops, or you can even stop short to rout a large curve on a counter top.

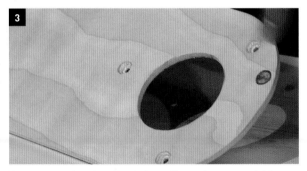

Routing large circles requires making a simple jig. This is a thin, narrow piece of plywood with a hole in the end.

The router attaches to the end of the jig. Use the router's removable base plate as a template to position the mounting holes in the jig.

Some router's mounting bolts will need countersinking.

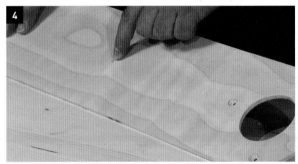

A pivot hole for a screw will be needed. It is drilled on the centerline of the jig and then positioned the distance from the router bit that is the size of the diameter of the circle.

To cut out a circle, use a straight bit and install it in the router.

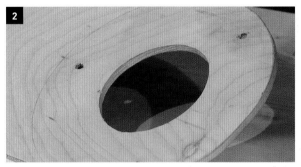

Prior to mounting the jig to the router, the router's base plate needs to be removed. This may have already been done to use it as a template for making the jig.

Invert the router and position the jig on the router's base to line up the mounting holes.

Tighten the mounting bolts securely to hold the jig firmly in place.

Turn the router back over and determine where the center of the cut is to be.

Then place a screw in the pivot hole and tighten it up...

...making sure that it is not so tight that the jig does not pivot...

...but tight enough so that the jig pivots evenly.

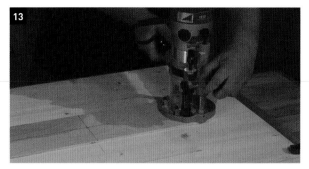

Set the depth of cut. Be aware that you may have to cut in two or more stages. The maximum depth of cut for a straight bit is the size of the diameter of the bit.

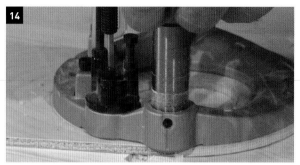

Start the router, plunge it to the first depth of cut, and proceed to rout the large circle in a counter-clockwise direction...

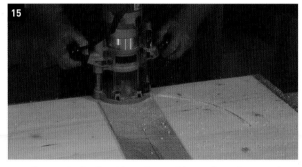

...so the router's direction of travel is against the rotation of the router bit.

Carry on routing the circle. You may need to reposition yourself and the power cord so it does not interfere with the path of the cut.

Keep on routing with a fluid movement until the whole circle is cut.

If deeper cuts are required to cut through the wood completely, reset the depth of cut and repeat the process until the cut goes through the wood.

When the large circle is cut, turn off the router and deplunge it.

Unscrew the pivot screw and remove it.

Move the router out of the way.

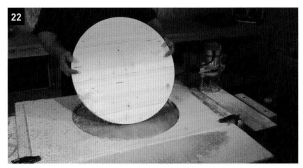

The large circle is now cut through completely and you can pick it up for inspection.

Turning it around will show that the cut is clean and the circle is smooth and even all round its circumference.

You can see the sacrificial board under the wood; this saves the bench being cut. If you wish to add an edge molding to the circle, the same jig can be used.

LARGE CIRCLE JIG

Routing large circles is easily done with another simple-to-make jig; once made, it can be modified to create circles of any size.

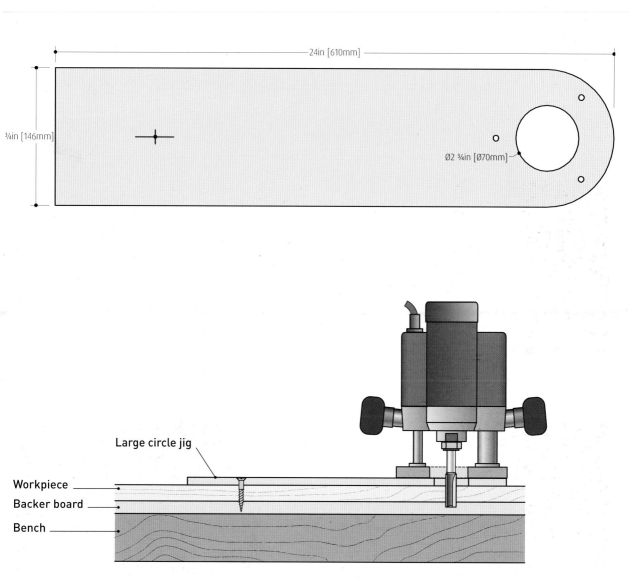

24in [610mm]

¾in [146mm]

Ø2 ¾in [Ø70mm]

Large circle jig

Workpiece

Backer board

Bench

Side view of large circle jig in use

ENTERTAINMENT UNIT FOR FLATSCREEN TV

This is a project to build an attractive and useful piece of furniture for the home using just the plunge router, a selection of router bits, a few simple jigs, and materials that are readily available from your local DIY store.

All the techniques used to make this piece are featured in this book, and are well within the abilities of the beginner router user.

CARCASS

The carcass of this unit is a large box with vertical dividers to isolate the center section for drawers, and two horizontal dividers for shelves. To start, all the components must be accurately cut to size. This is achieved using technique 1 (see page 32). The top and the bottom are the first pieces to cut to size; they are both exactly the same dimensions. Use a jigsaw to roughly cut them to length and then trim them to size using the router. The two vertical ends are cut to size next (refer to the drawing for the dimensions). These will be joined to the top and bottom with biscuit joints using technique 2 (see page 37). The two central dividers are slightly longer than the ends by ½in (12mm) to allow for the different joining technique. These will be fitted into ¼in (6mm)-deep dados in the top and bottom using technique 3 (see page 43). They will also need to be ¼in (6mm) less deep than the top and bottom to allow for the rabbet that will be cut in the other pieces later. The shelves are cut to length next. They are also fitted into dados, so make sure they are ½in (12mm) longer than the space between the vertical uprights. Once all these pieces are cut to size, the next thing to do is to join them. The vertical ends are joined to the top and bottom using biscuits. In this case there is enough room for three biscuits in each joint. Mark the position of the biscuits and proceed to make the joints as per technique 2 (see page 37).

The reason a dado is used for the vertical uprights is that it is not easy to create a biscuit joint midway on a board using a router. The dado is a simple joint, but careful measuring is required to make sure that the uprights are correctly placed. Remember that the top and bottom pieces are mirror images of each other. While cutting dados it is a good time to cut the ones for the horizontal shelves too. With all the dados, ensure that the cut stops short of the front edge to allow a step to be cut in the mating piece so the join does not show. Refer to technique 3 (see page 43). The last routing to do before assembly is the rabbet in the back edges of the top and bottom and the ends. Refer to technique 4 (see page 50) and cut the rabbets.

When all these joints have been cut, the carcass can be glued and assembled. It is a good idea to have some long clamps, and possibly an assistant available, as this is quite a large piece. If your clamps do not have soft jaws, you can cut small blocks of wood to put between the jaws and the carcass to stop it bruising when the clamps are tightened. I find it useful to lay the carcass on its front for the assembly process; this means it is also easier to make it square. Measure diagonally across the back of the carcass both ways. The measurements should be the same; if not, slacken the clamps and tap the carcass until they are, then retighten the clamps.

The backboard is a ¼in (6mm)-thick piece of plywood that sits in the rabbet routed in the back edges of the carcass. This means using technique 1 (see page 32) again to size the back and ensure it is a snug fit. However, before fitting, use technique 5 (see page 53) to rout a pair of small holes

The entertainment unit is just one of many pieces that can be made using the techniques outlined in this book.

Use the router to cut workpieces to size and true up their edges.

in the back to allow the power cables of your appliances to pass through. The position of the holes will depend on your appliances and the location of the power outlets. Once the small holes have been cut, simply drill and screw the back to the carcass. This will make the carcass extremely rigid.

BACK

The large vertical back not only makes the unit look substantial but allows some shelves to be added for easy storage of CDs or DVDs. The back is made up of three pieces; the center piece is wider than the outer two. The reason for this is that the center piece is left the width it is supplied in. The two outer pieces need to be cut to width, and all pieces are cut to the same length, using technique 1 (see page 32). The back pieces are attached together using biscuits; there is enough length for around six

of them. Mark their positions on all the pieces and then cut the joints using technique 2 (see page 37). The next step is to add an edge molding. As this is a plain piece of furniture, I decided to use a chamfer molding; you may decide to use an alternative one. Refer to technique 7 (see page 69) and follow the instructions for the correct sequence for routing to avoid tearout. The small shelves on either side of the back are fitted in using dados (technique 3, page 43), and then screwed in from the rear for extra rigidity. Cut the shelves to size using technique 1 (see page 32) and edge-mold them using technique 7 (see page 69). You will not need to worry about the back edge, as it will be hidden in the dado joint. Cut the dados in the back, making sure not to cut the full width of the shelf. This will allow notches to be cut, with a handsaw, in the shelf to hide the joint. When the dados have been cut, drill

Biscuit joints are used to make the carcass and drawer boxes.

Rout-stopped dados for the shelves and carcass dividers.

The small shelves are also fitted using dados. See how the notches in them cover the joint.

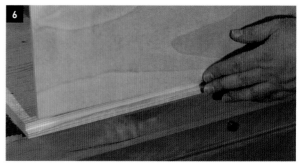

The backboard sits in a rabbet, which is routed on all the carcass back edges.

a couple of holes in them, place the shelves in the dados, and screw them in from the back. Now, put all the back pieces aside until later.

FEET

The feet look like large blocks of wood, but this is an illusion. They are really two pieces of wood joined together at right angles with a biscuit joint. The front piece is 2½in wide and ¾in thick (63mm by 19mm), so the return piece is 1¾in (44mm) wide to make both faces 2¾in (70mm). Cut them to size using technique 1 (see page 32). Put a single biscuit joint (technique 2, page 37) in the foot and glue them together. A square block is screwed in the top of the foot, which is then screwed into the carcass to hold the foot in place. Repeat this for all the feet.

DRAWERS

The drawers are simple boxes joined at their corners using biscuit joints. It is a good idea to buy the drawer slides you will be using prior to making the drawers, as this will ensure you get the drawer exactly the right size. Generally, the drawer slides require the drawer box to be 1in (25mm) narrower than the space it is to occupy. First, cut the drawer sides to the same length as the drawer slides using technique 1 (see page 32). Then cut the drawer fronts and backs to length, making sure that they are the width of the opening minus 1in (25mm) for the drawer slides and minus two thicknesses of the drawer sides. The drawer box is deep enough to place two biscuits in them, so cut all the joints for the three drawer boxes using technique 2 (see page 37). The bottom of the drawer is made from a piece of

Use the router and a simple jig to create the small holes for the appliances' power cables.

Screw the backboard in place on the back of the carcass to make the unit sturdy.

The tall back of the unit is attractive and is a good option for adding small shelves for DVDs or CDs.

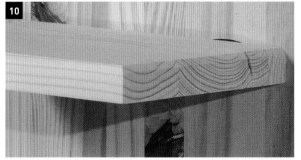

The small shelves on the back have a decorative chamfer around their front edges.

¼in (6mm)-thick ply. This simply needs screwing to the bottom of the drawer box, as it will mainly be hidden by the drawer slides.

The drawer slides need to be screwed into the carcass sides now. I decided to make all the drawer fronts the same width, so setting the position of the slides is easy. Measure the internal height of the carcass, then subtract the height of the drawer boxes times three. Divide the remaining measurement by three to get the gap size, and set the first drawer slide up from the bottom of the carcass by half of that gap measurement. The next drawer slide is fixed at one drawer height plus one and a half gaps, and the top drawer slide is fixed at two drawer heights plus two and a half gaps. This will space the drawers evenly. Also make sure the slides are fixed so their front is the thickness of the drawer front back from the front edge of the carcass. The drawer fronts are screwed to the front of the drawer boxes, so four holes need to be drilled in the front of the drawer box. Then the drawer fronts need to be cut to size using technique 1 (see page 32). The size of these needs to be the width of the opening minus the thickness of two pennies. Their height is the height of the opening minus four penny gaps then divided by three. I use pennies to set the gaps between the drawer fronts and the carcass as they are the right thickness and readily available. I decided to use a chamfer mold around the drawer fronts, as it hides any minor discrepancies in size. Simply use technique 7 (see page 69) to apply the molding around all of the drawer fronts. When the fronts are cut and molded, you will need to attach the handles of your choice to them from behind, unless you have front-fixing handles. Place two pennies side by side on the carcass

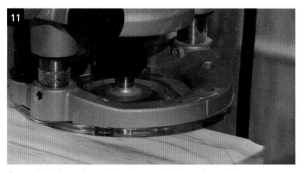

Rout the chamfer using the technique that will eliminate tearout.

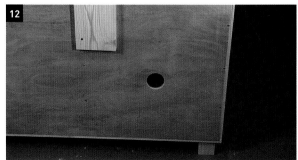

One of the small holes for the cables is seen here. See also the position of the feet and the brace that attaches the top to the carcass.

The drawer boxes are created using biscuits on all their corners.

Standard drawer slides are used to mount the drawers. You must allow for this thickness when making the drawer boxes.

floor and sit the bottom drawer front on them. Reach inside the drawer box and screw the front onto the box, making sure there is a penny gap either side too. Then put the second drawer box in place, put two pennies side by side on the top of the bottom drawer front, place the second drawer front on them, reach inside the drawer box and screw on the front.

The last front is slightly more difficult to attach, as you cannot reach into the drawer to screw on the front. Put the drawer box in the carcass, then place two pennies side by side on the top of the second drawer front. Now put a few pieces of thin double-sided tape on the front of the drawer box. Put the top drawer front onto the pennies and push it onto the drawer box. There will be enough stick with the double-sided tape to hold it there as you slide the drawer out, so you can screw on the front from inside the box.

FINISH

This is a simple piece of furniture that you can finish with a stain and varnish, or, if you to prefer to leave it the color it is, simply varnish it. You might also want to paint it to match your decor; either way it will look good. The last thing to do to assemble the unit is to sit the back pieces onto the top rear of the carcass and screw battens to the back of the carcass and also to the top backboards to hold them firmly in place. With this done, place all your electronic appliances in the unit and put it in place in your room.

The drawer boxes are tall enough to use two biscuits.

For a decorative effect, add a chamfer all around the drawer fronts.

Screw the drawer fronts to the drawer boxes to complete the project.

The finished entertainment unit will look good in any home.

ENTERTAINMENT UNIT
Exploded drawing

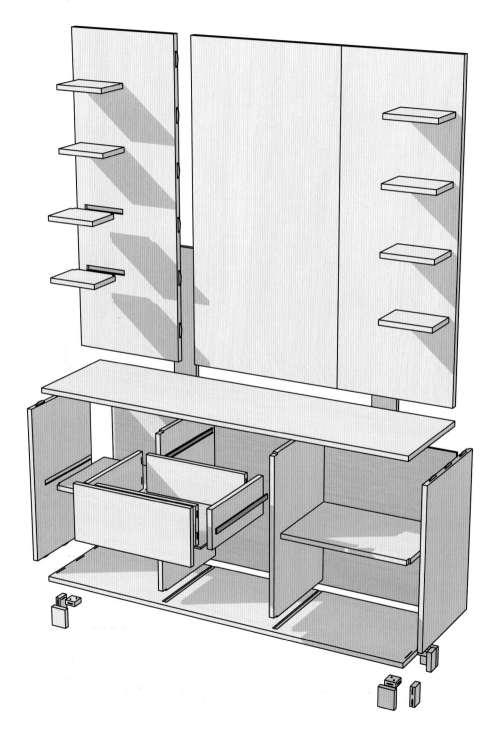

Dimension drawing

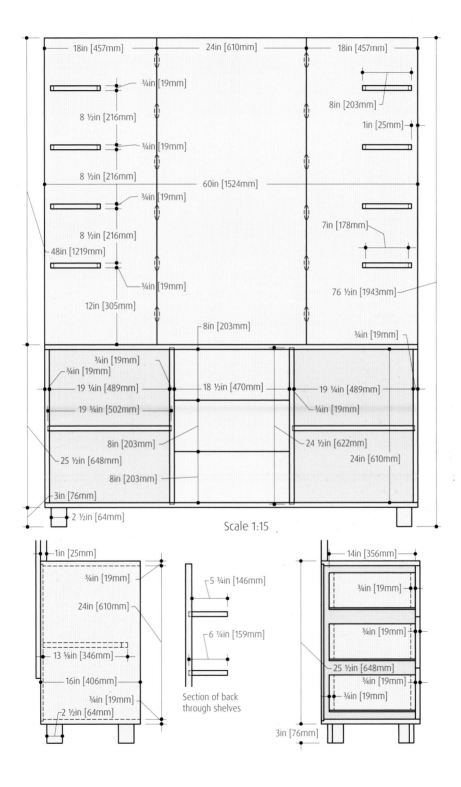

Scale 1:15

Section of back
through shelves

ROUND TABLE

This attractive table will be welcome in any home, and will also help you to improve your routing skills. Fire up the router and, with it, a few router bits and a few simple-to-make jigs you will soon have a piece of furniture to be proud of.

This useful piece of furniture is easily made using materials and hardware from your local home store. Making this table is an exercise in accurate routing, which will challenge your abilities but provide a satisfying and practical result.

TOP

The large round top is made from a piece of 1in (25mm)-thick pine board, using a simple jig that attaches to your router. The jig is easily made using a piece of thin plywood and shaped on the end to fit the router's base. First, cut a strip of plywood the same width as your router's base—in this case, 5¾in (146mm). Make it long enough to give a center point at least the radius of the circle you want to cut. Then the end of the jig needs to be formed to replace the standard base plate that comes with the router. The best way to do this is to use the base plate itself as a template. Remove it from the router and place it on the jig to mark the center hole and the holes to mount it on the router. Make sure you orientate the router the way you prefer; I like the handles to be at 90 degrees to the jig so I have more holding options when routing the circle. Screw the jig to the router and then measure the distance from the edge of the router bit to the center of the circle and mark it on the jig. Drill a hole on the mark. This is the pivot point. Screw the jig at this point into the underside of the top so the mark doesn't show. Proceed to rout the circle as per technique 8 (see page 76). You will no doubt want to put an edge molding on the top; a double Queen Anne molding is shown here. This process requires two different techniques to avoid putting a hole in the surface of the top. Place the Queen Anne bit in the router and set it to depth. Run the bearing on the tabletop edge and rout one side of the molding around the top edge of the top. To put the molding on the lower edge you will need to use technique 8 again (see page 76), as the bearing of the bit has nothing to run on now the top has been molded. Re-drill the pivot point on the circle jig to allow for the different diameter of the bit. Then proceed to cut the molding all round the edge of the top until the molding is complete.

BASE

The legs of the table could be square, but I decided to make the table a little more ornate and bought some ready-turned legs from the DIY store. If you have a wood lathe, you could turn the legs yourself. They do have square ends, however; these are required to make the mortise and tenon joints that hold the rails to them and support the top. We begin by cutting the rails to length using technique 1 (see page 32); it is useful in this project that they are all the same length. Next we create the edge bead molding on the bottom edge of the rails. Select the size of edge beading bit required and put it in the router. Set the router to depth so the bit will cut a small step on the top of the molding. Using technique 7 (see page 69), rout the molding on the edge of all the rails. Using the stacking technique as shown will give the router's base a wider platform to sit on and the operation will be more stable.

The next process involves making two simple jigs, probably from scrap wood you already have. Make the mortise jig from the piece of plywood that is the top plate that supports the

This round table is an easy project to make using a router, the techniques already described, and readily available materials.

Make a simple jig to help cut out large circles, and attach it to the base of the router.

base of the router. In this, rout a slot that is exactly the same width as a template guide. In this case, it is ½in (12mm). The slot must run parallel to the edge of the jig, but it can be longer than the mortise required as lines will be marked on the jig where their extremities are. On the underside of the jig's top plate a piece of batten is screwed—a distance away from the slot to where the mortise is to be routed. It must be parallel with the slot and at 90 degrees to the top plate. Remove the standard base plate from your router and replace it with one that accepts template guides. Fit the new base plate to the router and attach a template guide to it. The one selected here is a ½in (12mm) diameter one. Choose a straight router bit that has a diameter of about two-thirds the thickness of the rail and install it in the router, then set the depth of cut of the router for the first cut. Remember the maximum depth

of cut for a straight bit is the diameter of the bit, so if the bit is ¼in (6mm) diameter, cut a maximum of ¼in (6mm) deep. If your cut needs to be deeper, just reset the depth setting of the router to cut another ¼in (6mm) deep, and so on. Now rout the mortises as per technique 6 (see page 58). Repeat for the mortises in all the table legs, ensuring the two sides of the leg are mortised on the correct faces. The length of the mortise is easily determined by putting a pencil mark on the jig that lines up with the router's base at each end of the mortise and stopping the cut when these are reached.

Cutting the tenon in the rails also requires making a simple jig. It is very similar to the mortise jig, but performs a different purpose. There is a top plate for the router to run on and a batten underneath that is screwed on at exactly 90 degrees to the front edge and protruding beyond it at the

Screw the pivot point to the underside of the tabletop and cut the circle.

Complete cutting the circle all the way through the board. You then have a round tabletop.

Apply a Queen Anne edge molding on the top and bottom edge of the tabletop.

Rout an edge bead mold to the rails. Stack them in a vise to support the router base.

length the tenons need to be. The tenon cut is made using a dado bit, as this is wide with a flush bearing and has a bottom cut. Place the jig and rail into a clamp. Ensure the rail end lines up exactly with the end of the batten. Set the router to depth. This depth is cut on both sides of the rail, so some experimentation is required to get the thickness of the tenon to fit snugly in the mortise. When this is done, cut all the tenons as in technique 6 (see page 58). Make some test mortises on scrap wood first, to confirm that it is a good fit. Lastly, cut notches in the end of the tenons with a handsaw so the tenons allow the rail to align with the top of the legs.

FINISH

The final routing job is to make the blocks, or buttons as they are called, to hold the top onto the base. Make four blocks around 2in (50mm) long and ¾in (19mm) thick and rout a biscuit slot into their edge. Match the biscuit slot on the upper center of the rails. Lastly, drill a hole in the block to screw it to the tabletop. To fit the buttons, lay the top on a flat surface top down, then place the base onto it. Insert biscuits into the button's slots and place them in the slots in the rails. Then screw the buttons to the top to hold it to the base. There is no glue involved, as there will be some movement in the wood and the buttons need to be able to move slightly.

The last step is to stain and polish the finished table with your preferred choice of color and varnish, or leave a pine finish. Alternatively, paint the table to match your decor. Whatever your choice of finish you will have an attractive and practical table that will serve many purposes.

Fix the router base plate that accepts template guides to your router.

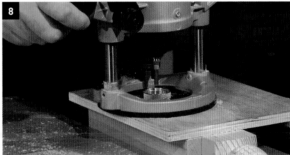

Using the simple mortise jig you have made, cut all the mortises in all the legs.

Cut the mortise so it is slightly narrower than the rail. This will allow for the tenon to be fitted exactly.

Make another simple jig; this time one for making tenons.

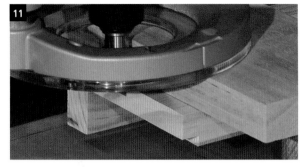

Cut one side of the tenon, then flip the rail over and cut the other side.

Adjust the depth of cut so that the tenon is a snug fit in the mortise.

Saw notches in the ends of the tenons to allow the top of the rail to be flush with the top of the leg.

The joint, with its edge bead molds, is both attractive and strong.

The table is both attractive and practical, and will look good in any home.

ROUND TABLE
Exploded drawing

Dimension drawing

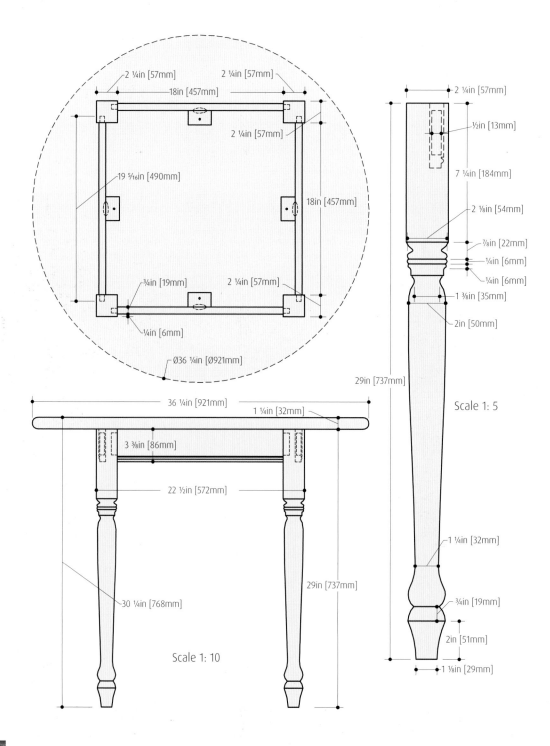

2 ¼in [57mm] 2 ¼in [57mm]
18in [457mm]
2 ¼in [57mm]
19 ⁵⁄₁₆in [490mm]
18in [457mm]
¾in [19mm] 2 ¼in [57mm]
¼in [6mm]
Ø36 ¼in [Ø921mm]

2 ¼in [57mm]
½in [13mm]
7 ¼in [184mm]
2 ⅛in [54mm]
⅞in [22mm]
¼in [6mm]
¼in [6mm]
1 ⅜in [35mm]
2in [50mm]
29in [737mm]
Scale 1: 5

1 ¼in [32mm]
¾in [19mm]
2in [51mm]
1 ⅛in [29mm]

36 ¼in [921mm]
1 ¼in [32mm]
3 ⅜in [86mm]
22 ½in [572mm]
29in [737mm]
30 ¼in [768mm]
Scale 1: 10

SAFETY ADVICE

Safety is the most important aspect of any woodworking procedure. You must follow some simple guidelines for your own safety, and always follow manufacturers' advice for the use of their tools. Routing is no exception, and you will need to take extreme care when using this power tool as well as any accessories that go with it.

Before changing router bits, or plugging in the router, always make sure the router switch is in the off position.

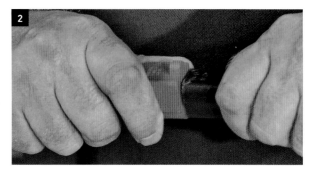

When working with the router for bit changing, setting depths, and installing accessories...

...always make sure the router is unplugged.

Before routing, check the power cable to ensure there are no breaks in it that would be a safety hazard or that might cause an electric shock.

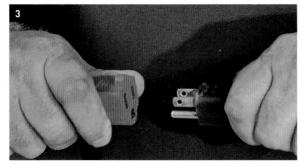

Inspect the power plug to ensure the pins are straight and in good condition.

Before commencing any power woodworking task, ensure that you remove rings, watches, and necklaces. These can get caught in tools and cause you harm.

Wear protective gear. Shown here is the minimum you will need for routing.

A dust mask will save your lungs from harmful dust. Ensure that you get one rated for the dust type produced for the material you are routing.

With this type of mask, it is essential to make sure the nose clip is tightened for a snug fit on your nose.

Safety goggles are a must, as a router can fling chips at your face at high speed. The goggles you use must be proper safety ones and be shatterproof.

When you put on the safety glasses, it is important that they fit correctly and completely cover your eyes.

Lastly, ear defenders will protect your eardrums from damage. Routers, especially when they are cutting, can produce ear-splitting noise.

GLOSSARY

BACKER BOARD
A board that is placed between a workpiece and the bench to prevent the bench from being damaged by cuts that go right through the workpiece.

BISCUIT JOINT
A slot cut into the edge of a board into which a plate or biscuit is inserted. When glue is applied the biscuit swells to create a tight joint.

CAPSTAN TURRET
A depth-stop device that has individually adjustable stops and can be rotated onto indents. Used for quickly setting predetermined depths of cut on a router.

CARBIDE TIPPED
Hard steel tips with sharp cutting edges brazed to cutting tools, such as saw blades and router bits.

CARCASS/CABINET
The case or box of a piece of furniture; it is the framework and structure of the item.

CHAMFER
A bevel on the edge of a board at a 45-degree angle.

COLLET
A type of chuck that accepts a fixed shank size, commonly used on routers.

COUNTERSINK
A drill bit that cuts an angle that allows a screw head to sit flush with the face of the material that it is driven into.

DEPTH STOP
A rod-type device on a router that bears onto the stops on a capstan turret.

FEATHERBOARD
A holding device with fingers used to hold a workpiece against a fence and/or down against the table on a tool such as a router table.

FENCE
A straight guide on a router table to keep the workpiece a set parallel distance from the bit.

FLUSH
When two adjoining surfaces are perfectly even with one another.

GRAIN
The appearance, size, and direction of the alignment of the fibres of wood.

GRIT
The grade of particles in sandpaper or sharpening stones that determines the aggressiveness of the cut.

GUIDE-BUSHES
A sleeve device that fits into a router's baseplate and controls the position of a router bit; typically used in conjunction with jigs.

JIG
A device used to hold work or act as a guide in manufacturing or assembly.

JIG SAW
A power tool that cuts by moving a blade up and down as it is guided through the cut.

MITER GAUGE
A guide with an adjustable head that fits in a slot and slides across a power tool table to cut material at an angle.

MOLDING
A piece of wood into which a shape has been cut with a router bit that has a specific profile.

MORTISE
The female part of a joint, which is a hole to accept a tenon, together forming a joint.

PARTICLE BOARD

A generic term for material manufactured from wood particles and bound together with glue.

PLUNGE BARS

The bars either side of a router that enable it to slide up and down.

PLUNGE ROUTER

A router that can be plunged down to quickly cut using a router bit.

PROUD

To just protrude above the surface so it is sticking out a bit.

RABBET

A groove in the edge of a board.

RAIL

A horizontal member between chair legs or between styles or vertical members of a door frame.

ROUTER

A high-speed motor with handles and an adjustable base with a collet that accepts profile bits to cut dados, rabbets, or shapes.

ROUTER BASE

Interchangeable plates that allow different functions for the router. One with a large hole allows large-diameter bits, and others have a hole that is designed to accept guide-bushes.

SIDE FENCE

A router accessory that attaches to the side of the router allowing cuts to be made a precise distance from the edge of a workpiece.

SOFT START

An electronic system on a power tool that controls the rapidity of the tool's acceleration to speed. On a router it tames the 'kick-back' that makes the router feel like it will pull from the hands.

SQUARE

An instrument used to layout or test right angles, with two arms at 90 degrees to each other. The longer and wider arm is the blade; the shorter, narrower arm is the tongue.

STILE

A vertical member of a door framework that is attached to the horizontal rails.

T-SLOT

A slot milled in the shape of an upside-down T to hold special bolts for clamps or jigs.

TABLE SAW

A circular saw mounted under a table with height and angle adjustments for the blade.

TEAROUT

The tendency to splinter the trailing edge of material when cutting across the grain.

TEMPLATE

A pattern to guide the marking or cutting of a shape. Often, a router is used with a piloted bit.

TENON

A projection made by cutting away the wood around it to insert into a mortise to make a joint.

VARIABLE SPEED

A device on a router to control the speed of the motor, enabling it to be slowed down for larger-diameter bits.

INDEX

Names of projects are printed in **bold**.

A

airflow 12
anatomy of a router 10–11

B

backer board 100
base plate 10
bases 10, 12, 15, 101
biscuit bits 23, 24
biscuit joining 37–42, 100
bits 8, 10, 17–24
    cleaning 26–7
    profiles 24
    removing 14
    sharp bits 26
    types of 17, 24

C

capstan turret 11, 13, 100
carbide tips 100
carcass/cabinet (definition) 100
chamfer bits 24
chamfers 84, 87, 100
chip deflector 11, 15
circles
    large 76–81
    small 53–7
cleaning bits 26–7
cleaning collets 26–7
cleaning work area 29
collets 10, 14, 100
    cleaning 26–7
countersink 100

D

dado bits 20–1, 24
dados 43–9
depth rod 11, 13
depth stop 100
downcut spiral straight bits 24
dust extraction 15, 30–1
dust masks 99
dust port 10, 15

E

edge bead bits 24
edge molding 69–75
    along an edge 70–1
    around an edge 72–4, 75
edge-molding bits 22
Entertainment Unit 82–9
    back 84–5
    carcass 83–4
    dimension drawing 89
    drawers 85–7
    exploded drawing 88
    feet 85
    finish 87

F

featherboard 100
fence 11, 14, 100
flush 100

G

grain 100
grit 100
guide-bushes 100
gyroscopic action 12

H

handles 12
holding work securely 29

J

jig saws 100
jigs 8, 100
    large circles 81
    small circles 57

K

knob-type handles 10, 11, 12

L

large circles 76–81
    jig 81

M

measuring 31
miter gauge 100
molding 100
mortise 100
mortise and tenon 58–68
    jig for mortise 67
    tenon jig 68
motor 12
motor body 12
motor brushes 10, 11
motor housing 10, 11

P

particle board 101

parts of a router 10–15

pattern bits 21, 24

plunge bars 10, 11, 101

plunge lock lever 10

plunge mechanism 13

plunge routers 8, 101

power cable 11, 28

practice cuts 30

pre-flight check 28

protective gear 99

proud 101

Q

Queen Anne bits 24

Queen Anne molding 91–2

R

rabbet bits 24

rabbets 50–2, 101

rails 101

Round Table 90–6

    base 91–2

    dimension drawing 96

    exploded drawing 95

    finish 93–4

    top 91

routers (definition) 101

rules for routing 25–31

S

safety 8, 97–9

    see also rules for routing

safety checks 27

shank of bit 18

side fence 101

small circles 53–7

    jigs 57

soft start 101

speed control 11, 13

speed scale 11

spindles 28

square 101

stile 101

straight bits 19, 24

straight edging 32–6

switch 10, 13

T

T-slot 101

table saw 101

tearout 101

templates 8, 101

tenon 62–6

tenons 101

trimming 32–6

U

up and downcut spiral straight bit 24

upcut spiral straight bits 24

V

variable speed 101

vents 11, 12

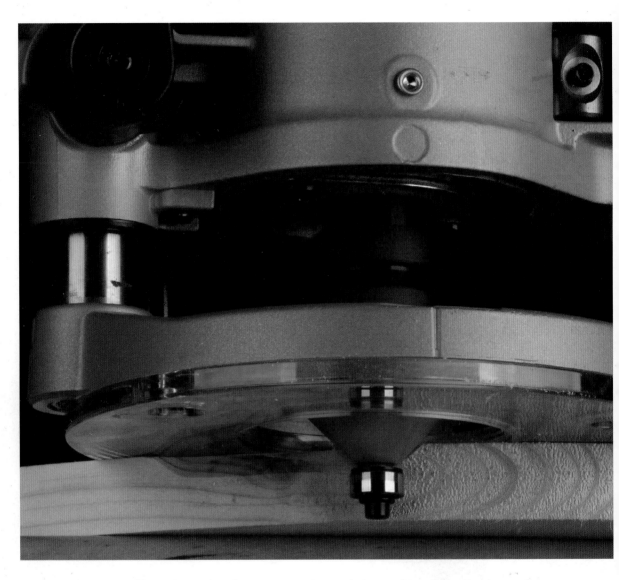

To order a book or request a catalog, please contact:

GMC Publications Ltd,
Castle Place, 166 High Street, Lewes,
East Sussex, BN7 1XU, United Kingdom

Tel: +44 (0)1273 488006
www.gmcbooks.com